Life Ground Rules

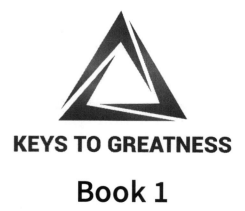

KEYS TO GREATNESS

Book 1

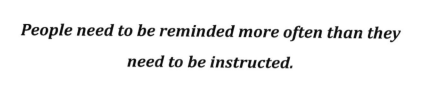

People need to be reminded more often than they need to be instructed.

– Samuel Johnson

Table Of Contents

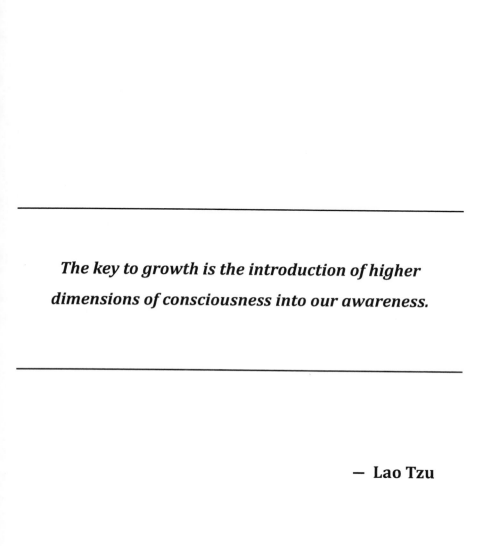

The key to growth is the introduction of higher dimensions of consciousness into our awareness.

— Lao Tzu

Introduction

L ife, in and of itself, is difficult. To further complicate things, there is no user's guide or life manual. However, opinions and advice are and have always been available. From a young age, we are told to listen to our parents, go to church, do good in school, seek higher education, get a job, or better yet, a career, get along, work well with others, get married, start a family, don't divorce, and be a productive member of society. Whatever that means. Yet despite following these instructions, we still experience heartaches and failures in one life area or another. We follow the instructions and advice provided yet still become victims to life's pitfalls. As a result, some of us end up empty and unsatisfied. Or worst yet, disgruntled and lost. Under these conditions, when faced with a crisis, it becomes difficult, if not impossible, to recover and move forward.

Why is it that even after following good advice, we still experience difficulties and sometimes feel purposeless? Answer— because there is no foolproof guidance on how to navigate through life. Besides the superficial, no one can tell us what to look for, who to avoid, or how to overcome specific experiences. As a result, we are unclear on how to best plot a course through our journey. Therefore, we figure things out through personal experiences, the hard way, usually at a steep price and late in life, if ever at all.

With the odds stacked against us, how can we win or even correctly play the game of life when we do not understand the rules? And yes, there are rules to this thing we call life.

In any event, rules provide a broader understanding of a "playing field." Rules can assist in directing activities to ensure we reach a desired or anticipated outcome. When understood and properly applied, rules provide awareness and confidence. They assure a likelihood, if not a sense of predictability, of what can or will happen when we follow or break a particular rule. Therefore, a rule, *any rule*, by its very nature, should be understood, considered, and properly applied. This principle cannot be overstated when referring to the rules of life.

A ground rule sets limits of understanding in life and provides basic principles of what to expect. These Ground Rules can guide future actions as they are simple to understand and easily applied unless we get distracted. This book explains and will show you how to **empower** yourself by utilizing the four ground rules that govern the general scope of our existence. The four Life Ground Rules are:

- Energy
- Human Polarity
- Same, Yet Different
- Ownership & Action

LIFE GROUND RULES

Human Energy

If you want to find the secrets of the universe,

think in terms of energy, frequency and vibration.

— Nikola Tesla

In life, energy is everything, and everything is energy. Energy can't be created, it's just there, and it is never lost; it merely dissipates or transforms. There are different types of energy: positive, neutral, and negative. All of which can be transformed from one form to another. Energy is also needed for all things to move, work, and change. Some forms of energy can be seen, while others are invisible. Whether visible or not, all energy moves in waves. These waves yield a frequency. Therefore, all types and forms of energy move with their unique wave frequency. These energy frequencies surround us and move through us. Through our minds and bodies. When energy is close or moving through us, its unique frequency produces a particular "feel." In certain circumstances, the feel of an energy frequency is responsible for what we call our "gut feeling." This gut feeling is what also gives us our intuition, defined as "the ability to understand something immediately, without the need for conscious reasoning."

Obviously, energy is essential because our bodies need and use energy to fuel each of our body systems and for our brains to function. The brain, although not the biggest organ, consumes the most energy. Why? Because the brain initiates everything, and everything starts with a thought. And here is where we enter the realm of human energy. Like a domino effect, thoughts trigger a unique mind-body energy chain of events. Thoughts give birth to ideas, beliefs, feelings, words and eventually, actions. And each of these steps, depending on what type of energy is used (positive or negative), will produce its distinctive frequency and feel, which at times, others can sense. Consequently, the type of energy we repeatedly consume and produce, over time, influences our thoughts. Our reoccurring thoughts will guide or determine the words we use and, ultimately, our actions.

Mind-Body Energy Chain

This mind-body energy chain, which moves us from thoughts to actions, manifests itself in the following manner:

- Thoughts

   Thoughts are ever-flowing, and the majority are involuntary. The mind can have thousands of thoughts during the day and more while we sleep. Some spontaneous thoughts can be intrusive and unrelated to anything that we have been thinking about at the moment. Some intrusive thoughts can be right-out inappropriate— according to society's standards. However, the sum of all our thoughts creates ideas and mental visions. Due to this, it is critically important to be mindful of our frequently repeated thoughts. Don't let your thoughts guide your life. Learn to control and direct your thoughts.

   Meditation and affirmations help. Do what you must to manage your thoughts to reduce fears, anxiety, and stress. Focus on goals and the positive things in your life. Eventually, controlling your thoughts will produce your desired results.

- Ideas

Ideas, whatever they may be, establish opinions and perceptions, which then influence how we think and view things. Unfortunately, many of our ideas were not created by us. Instead, they were given or passed down to us by someone else. Nevertheless, whether original or not, consistent ideas fashion our belief system.

- Beliefs

What we believe solidifies our viewpoint. This is how perceptions become reality. Thereby, it is imperative that we try to view things from all possible angles because what we see and then believe to be factual, whether accurate or not, becomes our reality. Beliefs also help produce feelings, emotions, and moods, which are the physical manifestation of our thoughts and ideas.

- Feelings

Being mindful of and being able to control your feelings is probably one of the most crucial life skills. He or she who can manage their feelings can master their life. Because feeling can intensify anything. Emotions give depth to our words and establish our speech patterns. The more feelings in our words, the more truthful they are to us. This is how feelings give validity to words, regardless of whether the words are true or not. The more emotions in our speech, the more we convince ourselves and others of those statements.

LIFE GROUND RULES

- Words

Words have the power to motivate, encourage and impact our conscious minds. Consistent words backed by passionate beliefs influence our subconscious, which is how we eventually create or change our own reality. This is how we change the world around us, or at least how we view it. Unfortunately, many of us don't pay close attention to the words we use, especially those used to describe ourselves and our situations. Words have power. Use it wisely.

- Action

Action is king! Words can be powerful, but nothing happens without action. Whether done consciously or subconsciously, consistent actions create habits. And habits can build or destroy a person. So if you want something done, take action.

Watch your thoughts, they become words. Watch your words, they become actions. Watch your actions, they become habit.

— **Laozi**

LIFE GROUND RULES

With the correct type of energy and minimal interruptions, the mind-body energy chain moves us from thought to words and into action. Consistent actions create habits. Ultimately, steady habits shape our lives. Unfortunately, many of us do not use our minds. Instead, we let our minds use us. Worst yet, many misuse their minds to validate made-up fears, to repeatedly think about a guilty past, or to anxiously worry about the future. This misuse of the mind can become a habit. A habit we are not aware of.

Forming Habits

Regarding consistent actions, it takes 21 to 31 days to establish a physical habit. Additionally, a consistent way of thinking adjusts our subconscious, and remember, the subconscious mind characterizes our existence. This makes understanding and knowing how to properly use the subconscious mind so important. Yet, unlike a physical habit, it takes 120 to 190 consistent and uninterrupted days of thinking and believing in something to alter our subconscious. Therefore, to change how we think and act, we must adjust our thoughts. To transform our lives, we must change our habits. And to change the way we see and interact with the world around us, we must adjust our subconscious mind. Change and improvement are possible, but there are obstacles.

The biggest obstacle to mental and physical change is distractions. In our current world, we are surrounded by numerous distractions and things that continually fight for our attention. For example, we are constantly bombarded with information, advertisements, and attention-grabbing entertainment that waste our time. And if we don't plan our day or organize our lives, we let time slip away. Time is the only thing in this world that we cannot buy or make more of. It is a precious commodity that we must not waste on unproductive actions. Unproductive actions are activities that don't benefit us and, in the long run, can be detrimental. Eventually, an excess of unproductive actions can negatively impact our mind-body energy chain. As a result, our precious time is lost, and our valuable human energy is wasted. Just like time, human energy is limited and, therefore, must be valued and protected.

The 8 Fundamentals

Most types of human energy can be easily influenced and disturbed. So, as we create habits and regulate our subconscious thinking, we must remain aware and well-grounded. This ensures that we generate precious human energy and use it wisely. The best way to stay on course is to establish a solid life Foundation. A life Foundation consists of eight basic yet extremely important activities. If done consistently, these actions have a dynamic impact on our life. In fact, these basic yet effective principles must be incorporated into our daily routine if we seek to live the best life possible.

The 8 Fundamentals are Sleep – Focus – Water – Diet – Exercise – Avoid – Consistency – and Lifestyle. Here is a brief description of each of the 8 Fundamentals:

LIFE GROUND RULES

- Sleep: Getting sufficient, regularly scheduled sleep is necessary to recharge the mind and body. Make it a goal to set a consistent sleep schedule that allows you 6 to 8 hours of sleep daily. With that being said, allow sufficient time so you can wake up an hour or two earlier than usual to conduct a Focus Session or a morning routine. This is "me" time. The time you allocate for yourself to calm your mind and focus your life. This is when you *empower* your mind, body and spirit.

- Focus: A Focus Session is a specified period one spends alone to get mentally focused, physically strong and spiritually balanced. This is time for yourself. A Focus Session can last 15 minutes to an hour or more if you incorporate exercise. Preferably, it is best to do it first thing in the morning. Focus Session activities can consist of breathing, meditating, affirmations, gratitude, reviewing your life purpose and goals, reading, and exercising. It can include any activity that helps you improve and develop. Just like a workout program, you should conduct a Focus Session 3 to 5 times per week, if not daily.

- Water: There are so many benefits to keeping the body hydrated. Therefore, we should drink enough water. Yet it is hard to find a definitive answer on what is enough. So, this is what I recommend, drink at least 32 to 64 ounces of water daily. Adjust your intake depending on your body type, size, weight, and activity level. The objective is to benefit from drinking sufficient water without it being an inconvenience.

- Diet: By "diet," I am referring to a good eating plan and not necessarily cutting calories. We all know that maintaining a healthy diet is vital for overall health and to prevent diseases. Although we know this, the hard part is actually doing it. The expansion of the fast-food industry makes it even harder. Therefore, it will require a degree of discipline. Do what you must to eat a clean, balanced diet. It may require that you prepare your meals in advance and avoid processed foods.

- Exercise: The benefits of exercising are obvious. Set a schedule to exercise 3 to 5 days per week, if not more. An exercise session can last 15 minutes to an hour. Within your exercise routines, incorporate compound movements and functional training. Don't limit or stagnate your exercise routines. Instead, mix it up, challenge yourself and try something new. Incorporate strength training, cardiovascular training, and movements that improve your flexibility and mobility.

- Avoid: These are the things that must be avoided if you really want to make progress. Because even when you are taking the right actions, there will be things, people, activities and places that will hinder your progress. These things will negatively influence you, interrupt your flow and disturb your energy. That being the case, when changing or improving your life, all interruptions and negativity must be avoided. In general, avoid stress, distractions, negativity, unproductive actions, procrastinating, gossip, and fast food. By stress, I am referring to any unnecessary drama that can be avoided. Additionally, remove any negative distractions, things that can be detrimental to your growth and junk food from your home.

- Consistency: Absolutely nothing works without consistency. Hence, you must be consistent with your actions so you can create solid habits. If you skip or mess something up, don't give up. Don't surrender the rest of your day just because of one or two mistakes. Keep going. Even after failure, get back up. Understand that true success and greatness require sacrifice, hard work, discipline, and consistency. Balanced consistency is key!

- Lifestyle: This is not a fad; it is a warrior-monk way of life. This Foundation works only if you commit to them. Only if you are serious about it. To do that, you have to eliminate stress, clutter, and disorder from your life and make these principles a lifestyle— a clean, active, and balanced lifestyle with plenty of outdoor activities. Applying these 8 Fundamentals is a way of life in which you take action daily to learn, grow, and further develop your mind, body, and spirit. It is a lifestyle where you find ways to challenge and improve yourself. Where you learn from your mistakes, establish goals, work hard, stay focused and move forward. Above all else, it is a lifestyle that allows you to enjoy your journey.

Success is neither magical nor mysterious.
Success is the natural consequence of consistently
applying the basic fundamentals.

— **Jim Rohn**

Energy Harmony

As you implement these eight fundamentals into your life, remain aware not to compromise your energy harmony. Understand that all things in your life are interconnected. Even the things that initially appear to be opposite to each other, like good and bad or hard and soft. All things and all forms of energy are needed to establish and maintain balance in your life. At first glance, these things may seem to be opposites that contradict each other, so you'll have a natural inclination to mentally separate them. This way of thinking may prevent you from having balance. Instead of separating them, find ways in which seemingly different things can work together and complement each other. This is especially the case when dealing with hard and soft energy.

Here are examples of basic hard and soft energies so you can better understand what I am referring to.

Soft Energy	Hard Energy
Negative	Positive
Feminine	Masculine
Cold	Hot
Soft	Hard
Slow	Fast
Relaxed	Intense

Everything in the Universe requires both hard and soft energy. The two are needed to maintain harmony in the cosmos. Hard and soft energy are necessary for everything that exists, including the human mind, body, and spirit. Hard and soft energy is also needed to synchronize all that we do and to provide balance to everything in our life. This is true for both men and women. Traditionally, men have been associated with hard energy and women as soft. But that should not always be the case. And to make it crystal clear, I do not agree with this new liberal way of thinking where men are demonized, and masculinity is considered toxic. I am a man and consider myself a professional warrior. Remember, that samurai warriors practiced soft arts such as Zen, brush painting, and mastered tea ceremonies. That was their way of maintaining balance and addressing the ugly stresses of war; what is now commonly known as post-traumatic stress disorder (PTSD). And we can't forget women's contribution and hard work during World War I and more so during the 2nd World War. In fact, biologically speaking, most women can birth a child, but being a good mother is not for the weak. So, regardless of who you are or what you do, energy harmony, or the lack thereof, impacts what we do and everything in our life.

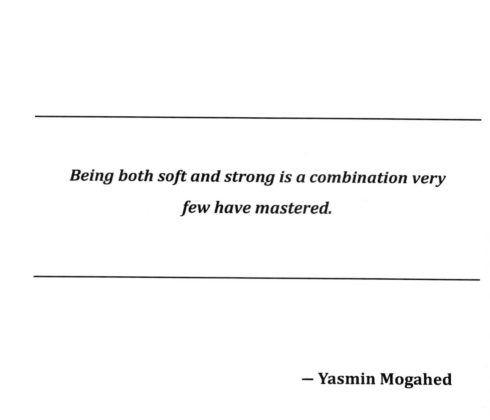

Being both soft and strong is a combination very few have mastered.

— Yasmin Mogahed

It is obvious that hard and soft energy are on opposite sides of the energy scale, with neutral energy sitting somewhere in the middle. Although these two forms of energy appear to be on the extreme spectrum of each other, we need both in life to equalize things. If something is off in your life, more than likely, it is due to a lack of balance. This is why there must be a harmonious interaction between soft and hard energies to stabilize and maintain balance in life. In book three of this series, life balance and how to achieve it is covered in greater detail.

In addition to helping establish life balance, and more importantly, each type of energy helps foster their respective skill sets. Therefore, with awareness and some effort, we can acquire both hard and soft skills. This may be the first time that some readers have heard about the notion of hard and soft skills. Yet the willingness to mentally accept this concept and the inclination to physically learn these skills will help achieve balance and improve the quality of your life.

The Harmony Between Hard & Soft Skills

The differences between the two skill sets (hard skills and soft skills) are not conflicting forces. On the contrary, they actually complement each other. Together they are essential to realizing and sustaining a wholesome life. To those who don't understand or accept this concept, I ask that you please keep an open mind and bear with me. Soon you will see how these skills are necessary to excel in life and the importance of learning, acquiring, and mastering them both. Now, let's look at each skill set more closely.

Hard Skills

Hard skills are the abilities needed to perform or complete a task, whether in a group or alone. It provides the capacity to do something well. Hard skills can usually be identified and gauged by capabilities or by formal training. People with advanced hard skills are sought for their knowledge and abilities on a particular subject matter or for their capacity to perform a given task. Hard skills are necessary to work effectively, get a job, establish a career, become a professional, and to live out your life purpose. A good worker has solid hard skills. Yet, a good leader requires soft skills.

Soft Skills

By contrast, soft skills are usually tricky to measure. Soft skills are not seen, but they are felt. These are the interpersonal skills that attract others to you. People with soft skills are patient and have empathy which makes them good listeners and communicators. They are easy to be around, and they get along well with just about anyone. Those with soft skills encourage team cohesiveness which increases productivity. As it relates to any job or career field, a person with hard skills will require soft skills to further excel in their profession or to move into leadership positions. Another way to see this concept is that people with hard skills can manage things, and those with soft skills can manage and lead people.

The Problem in Neglecting Either Skill

Problems and difficulties arise related to these skill sets when individuals rely solely on hard skills and neglect soft ones. This usually results in a good worker who typically has a hard time getting along or working well with others. On the flip side, and worst yet, is when workers lean on their excellent people skills to the point where they no longer practice their talents, they become non-proficient and finally incapable. Usually, these unskilled individuals eventually get intimidated by those with hard practical skills. Ironically, these incompetent individuals still rise into leadership positions. Unfortunately, these people tend to promote like-minded individuals and those they are comfortable with. This is how an organization ends up with an inept top management team. A trend that can ultimately damage an organization. To prevent this from happening, promotion requirements should not be subjective wherever possible. For those reasons, having both types of skills is critical. The good news is that both hard and soft skills can be learned, practiced, and improved.

When taking stock of your job, career, or any upward mobility goals, your capabilities in hard and soft skills should be examined. If you are lacking in anything or if there is room for improvement, take the actions necessary to improve. There are books, courses and mentors that can help you improve any skill. You just have to be willing to learn.

LIFE GROUND RULES

Yet, regardless of your occupational role, understand that you are the leader of your life and living life to the fullest is your primary profession. And being good at this profession entails hard and soft skills. Why? Because this unique profession requires specific actions to develop good habits in every aspect of life. To perform these actions consistently, you need sufficient energy. So, the more energy you have, the more you can do.

Consequently, the more you do, the more hard and soft skills you develop. Hence, the circle of life. This is what is meant to live life to the fullest. In the long run, these hard and soft skills are necessary to sustain a happy, fulfilled, and successful life. Working together, these skills allow you to be gainfully employed. They are also needed if you want to start a business or pursue your life purpose. With sufficient energy and the right balance, you'll be able to do all these things while getting along with others. This allows you to improve relationships. As a result, you will network better and, at the same time, minimize conflicts and reduce stress. Therefore, the quality of your professional and personal life directly correlates with your ability to acquire hard and soft skills, and with the amount of your physical and mental energy. So, we must do all we can to generate human energy, use it efficiently, and protect it at all costs.

A man doesn't need brilliance or genius, all he needs is energy.

— **Albert M. Greenfield**

Life Application

The following is a review of the information covered in this section that can serve as reminders. And it includes some examples and tips on how you can practically apply these concepts in your life.

- Understand that energy is in everything. Therefore everything is energy. Energy vibrates and moves in waves which creates a unique frequency.

- Everything is energy, including your thoughts, ideas, beliefs, feelings, words, and actions (the mind-body energy chain). And each of these has its unique frequency, which at times, you and others can feel. This is why you can't ignore how the energy around you feels. Pay attention to the vibes you get from people, places and situations. If it doesn't feel right, it probably isn't.

- Everything starts with a thought, so remain aware of what you contemplate and of your thinking pattern. Make an effort to think positively. Don't be naïve; expect the best and prepare for the worst. In every situation, come in peace, but be ready for war. Yet always lean towards being more optimistic. It's the healthier choice.

- Meditating regularly is one of the best methods to remain aware of your thoughts. In addition, daily affirmations are critical to adjust your subconscious. And expressing gratitude helps keep a positive mindset.

- To change the way you see the world around you, adjust your thoughts. To transform your life, change your habits. Remember that distractions are the biggest obstacle to change, so eliminate them wherever possible.

- Due to various distractions, your energy and thoughts can be easily influenced and disturbed. As a result, you must create good habits and regulate your subconscious to remain well-grounded.

- The best way to remain well-grounded is to establish a daily/morning routine that incorporates the 8 Fundamentals: **Sleep** – **Focus** – **Water** – **Diet** – **Exercise** identify things to **Avoid** – Be **Consistent** – and make it a **Lifestyle**.

- Both hard and soft energy are needed for everything in our lives and in all that we do. A combination of soft and hard energy is necessary to maintain peace and harmony. This is part of having balance in life.

- These two forms of energy help produce their respective skill sets.

- Hard skills are the abilities needed to perform or complete a task. These skills provide you with the capacity to do something well.

- Soft skills allow you to develop interpersonal skills that attract others to you. These skills make you a better listener and communicator.

- Learn Hard skills and Soft skills; both are necessary to succeed and sustain a good life.

- The more energy you have, the more you can do. So, the quality of your life directly correlates with the value and amount of the physical and mental energy you possess.

- Do everything possible to create positive energy, use it efficiently, and protect it at all costs.

The longer I live, the more deeply I am convinced

that that which makes the difference between

one man and another-between the weak and

the powerful, the great and the insignificant, is

energy-invisible determination-a purpose once

formed and then death or victory. This quality will

do anything that has to be done in the world, and

no talents, no circumstances, no opportunities,

will make one a man without it.

— **Sir Thomas Buxton**

LIFE GROUND RULES

Human Polarity

But there is no energy unless there is a tension of opposites; hence it is necessary to discover the opposite to the attitude of the conscious mind.

— C.G. Jung

P olarity is the relationship between two opposite characteristics or trends within a single field or body. By definition, "it is the state of having two opposite or contradictory tendencies, opinions, or aspects." Polarity exists in all things within the universe, including life itself. It also exists within the human mind, body, and spirit— within your inner being. Polarity refers to the full spectrum of human behaviors and capabilities in both men and women. It indicates our two most outer limits that reside within each of us. Human Polarity states that everyone possesses the two poles or opposite points of whatever is possible within the human psyche. We all possess the two extremes of good and evil within. No matter who or what you are, everyone is capable of good and evil.

From a young age, we are taught that there are good people and bad people. As we grow older, we continue to categorize people subconsciously as either good or bad. This separatist form of thinking indicates that certain people can be trusted while others should be avoided. If we expand this viewpoint, we can justify identifying a group of people, certain neighborhoods, or even an entire race as good or bad.

Based on cultural norms, the definition of a good person may vary slightly. Yet, generally speaking, a good person behaves well within societal norms. They are respectful towards others, truthful, authentic, kind, giving, and reliable. A good person is not a burden to society because they are competent, skilled, helpful and valuable in one way or another. Good people are also considered to be moral, virtuous, and pleasant to be around.

On the other hand, exists the corrupt, the improper, and those who have turned away from what is viewed as right and good. If we continue to travel down this dark path, we will find the bad and wicked. Those who harm others and display the type of human behaviors that stray from that which is accepted as normal and conventional. If we continue further, we find the evil and perverse— those who, either publicly or privately, display mostly neurotic, abnormal, or vile behaviors.

Consequently, and once again, based on our upbringing, cultural norms, and opinions, everyone falls under one of these two categories. Either good or bad. If this is how we see the world, then Human Polarity goes against what most have learned. Because of this, initially, many people find it difficult to accept this ground rule. Yet the reality is that there are no such things as good people or bad people. The truth is that the extremely good and pure, as well as the exceptionally evil and perverse, lives within us all. We are all capable of being good and evil.

That being the case, there are no good people or groups of bad people. Instead, we are all a combination of the two, and most of us fall somewhere in the middle of this spectrum. The vast majority of us are simply people who do some good things and some bad things. At times, people with good moral fiber do evil things. Similarly, unethical people are capable of kind acts. This means that everyone can be either the hero or the villain in any given situation— at any stage of life. Anyone can be tremendously good or unusually wicked; whether or not you publicly display your actions or are willing to admit it is another discussion.

Nonetheless, although most of us fall somewhere in the middle, we will gradually lean to one side or the other. The side we lean towards is based on our overwhelming habits and the sum of what we consume mentally. Yet, since *Human Energy* can be refocused and how *Human Polarity* functions, it is possible that a villain can consistently perform good acts and even transform into a hero. Similarly, a hero can do evil deeds and mutate into a villain. Becoming or remaining a hero or a villain depends on what we focus on. The outcome is based on what we gravitate towards. If our conscious thoughts, ideas, beliefs, feelings, words, and actions are primarily good, we **empower** the hero within us. On the other hand, if our mind-body energy chain is predominantly negative and wicked, don't be surprised when the villain within emerges.

People, Places & Things

With that being said, try to remain aware of the people you surround yourself with. Be cognizant of the places you frequently visit and of the things you routinely do. Most importantly, be mindful of the things you think about that ultimately, and at times unconsciously, become habits. Try to remain aware of these things and adjust when you need to. If you mess up, fail, or have a bad day or even a bad week, don't give up. Get back up and try again. As quoted by Chris Mentillo, *"Don't let your past dictate your future."* So don't let a mistake you made an hour, a day or a week ago dictate your future performance and outlook on life. No one is perfect, and our goal should be to become better than we were yesterday. With time and practice, it becomes a way of life. A lifestyle in which the aim is to be the very best hero possible. Once achieved, our goal then becomes to continue being a hero. Human Polarity makes this goal feasible.

And don't misunderstand what being a hero means and requires. Being a hero doesn't mean that you have to be a pushover. It doesn't require that you be a punching bag for others to abuse. You don't have to turn the other cheek. Remember, expect the best but be prepared for the worst. Come in peace but stay ready for war. Ironically enough, being a nice person who clearly displays that you won't be bullied is the best way to avoid most conflicts.

The bottom line is that our *Human Polarity* is determined by which side, the hero or the villain within, we feed and nurture the most. It is based on the type of energy we primarily consume and surround ourselves with. On what we habitually think and focus on. Therefore, Human Polarity is influenced and depends on what we consistently provide our mind, body, and spirit.

No tree, it is said, can grow to heaven unless its roots reach down to hell.

— **Carl Jung**

Life Application

The following is a review of the information covered in this section that can serve as reminders. These are also ways in which you can better manage the concept of *Human Polarity* within yourself and how to address it in others.

- Never forget that everyone, yes everyone, has good and evil within.

- Approach everyone you meet, all situations, and all relationships with this understanding.

- Be more understanding and willing to forgive because those we may consider good people sometimes do bad things. Similarly, "bad people" are capable of moral and kind acts.

- Everyone is capable of good and evil, so as the Russian proverb goes, "*trust but verify*".

- Have faith in everyone and in everything. Anticipate that everyone will be good to you but confirm their honesty and their intent. How? Ask them. This may be uncomfortable to do, but well worth it.

- Trusting and verifying requires open, honest, and upfront communication. Yet understand that although your questions may be honest and upfront, the responses you receive may not. Feel the energy.

- In all situations, expect the best but be prepared for the worst.

- In any conflict, ask for peace, but be ready for war. In any mental, physical, or spiritual battle, hit first, hit hard, and hit fast.

- After the offensive, defend and protect yourself at all times.

- If offended or violated, you can, and you should forgive, but keep your distance.

- Understand that you are neither inherently good nor evil. Instead, you have both good and evil within you.

- The identity that lives within, the hero or the villain, depends on what you focus on and what you constantly feed your mind, body, and spirit.

- Being a hero doesn't mean that you have to be a pushover.

- The best way to avoid conflict is to be a nice person who can display that they won't be bullied.

- Establish a morning/daily routine that feeds and nurtures the superhero within you.

Everybody has a little bit of the sun and moon in them. Everybody has a little bit of man, woman, and animal in them. Darks and lights in them... No one exists without polarities. Everybody has good and bad forces working with them, against them, and within them.

— Suzy Kassem

LIFE GROUND RULES

Same, Yet Different

You have your way. I have my way. As for the right way, the correct way, and the only way, it does not exist.

— **Friedrich Wilhelm Nietzsche**

We are all the same, yet we are different. This Ground Rule may seem simple, if not elementary, yet for that reason, it is usually misunderstood and rarely applied. Yes, as people or as collective groups, we are all the same. We can argue whether hundreds or thousands of years ago, 10 or 21 other human species may have existed before, but now, we must agree that we are all from the same, single species. The human species. Although diverse, we are all still humans living on the same planet. We all have similar needs, wants, and desires. We all want to be treated well, and in our own way, we all want to be successful in whatever we do and live happy and fulfilled lives. The similarities among us, even between totally different cultures around the world, cannot be denied. We all seek to be successful, happy and fulfilled.

Now, although we are similar in those aspects, we are all different because everyone's description of success and sense of happiness is different. What fulfills one person may be a burden for another. These differences in how we define what makes us content may be found among people within the same group. This is the case with individuals from the same country, neighborhood or even within the same household. We are all on the road of "life," seeking success, happiness and fulfillment. But everyone's destination and "mode of travel" are different. Therefore, everyone's voyage, experiences, and perspectives will be different.

Accordingly, when discussing the meaning of our life journey, there is no single definition to adhere to. There is no single path for all of us to take. The only thing that is certain for us all, is that we all need and want some form of Direction and Balance. Yet how we determine our life's direction and establish that balance is up to each of us. Because in all aspects of life, there is no one solution for everyone. There is no such thing as "a way" for us all. This concept applies to almost all things in life. The magic pill does not exist. There is no single diet, no single exercise program, no single supplement, treatment, medication, religion, or daily routine that works for everyone. Whatever advice, method or technique that works well for you, may not work for someone else.

This fact has nothing to do with the technique, or with the instructions, or even with the method being used. It has more to do with our individuality. It has everything to do with how any given method or technique is applied. Yes, most things can work for us, but some may require modification to function for our individual minds, body, and spirit. For most things in life, the general concept may be the same, but how we understand, accept, and apply it, is different.

Discover Your Own Path

Although we are all the same in that we are all trying to reach our destination, we are different because we must individually get there using our own means and methods. We need to independently discover, identify, and take our distinctive path to arrive at whatever we are trying to achieve. If not, you'll be walking along someone else's journey, and you won't be satisfied with what you get out of life. This is the case because we are all individually unique. Therefore, we must take active ownership of our own lives to ensure we create and live the life we want. This is the key to finding our Direction and establishing our own Balance. This duty and responsibility fall on our shoulders alone. This is one thing that we cannot surrender if we want to be satisfied in life. We cannot freely accept the ideas, concepts, methods, teachings, and advice of others without considering our unique individuality.

What I refer to as our individuality, is our essence. We must understand what our essence is and learn how to apply it in life. This undertaking takes work. It requires awareness and effort. Without awareness and the willingness to invest effort in ourselves, we get mentally lazy. And just like everything else, allowing ourselves to become mentally lazy can become a habit. With a lazy way of thinking, we just follow the crowd. We begin to freely accept the words and opinions of others without honestly considering our individual uniqueness. The sad thing is that we sometimes do this unconsciously at the expense of our happiness or other personal costs. We do things without considering what satisfies us and what makes us happy as an individual. Then we wonder why we feel incomplete or empty. So, we run off looking for someone else's guidance or for something else that can fill us. Stop running and looking for something else. Whatever you are looking for or need resides within you. Stop, calm the mind and search for it. You will find it. This is the critical element of this ground rule. We are all the same, yet we are individually different. And this difference lies within.

And lastly, this Ground Rule (*Same Yet Different*) should not be misunderstood or used as an excuse to dodge the things that are difficult yet necessary in life. Although we are all unique, the only element that doesn't change is that sacrifice, hard work, discipline, and consistency are required by anyone trying to accomplish anything meaningful in life. We may face different challenges, but the formula to overcome them is the same for us all. So stay strong and live hard.

Life Application

The following is a review of the information covered in this section that can serve as reminders and tips. These can help you better understand the ground rule of *Same Yet Different* and how it can be best applied in your life.

- There is no single definition for the purpose or meaning of life. The only constant is that we all need and want some form of Direction and Balance.

- There is no single path for all of us to take. You must define your Direction and Balance.

- In all difficult life situations and obstacles, there is no one solution for everyone. Good advice may work, but it may not apply to us all. Modification may be required.

- The magic pill does not exist. No single thing will, in and of itself, improve your life. Instead, self-improvement and personal development require doing several things for some time. Improving as a person entails taking an active and holistic mind, body, and spirit approach.

- By "active", I mean that you need to take action while remaining aware to see what works and what needs modification. By "holistic", I am referring to collectively improving and maintaining a strong mind, body and spirit. For example, read, exercise and meditate at least five days per week.

- Understand that no single diet or exercise routine works for everyone. A particular diet may work for your friend but not for you. It's not the diet that determines whether or not it works; it's your individual body makeup and how you apply it that will determine its effectiveness.

- No single exercise program, no single supplement, treatment, or single medication works for everyone. Try everything, give it an honest effort, don't give up, and remain aware to see what works for you and what doesn't. More importantly, be mindful to see what needs to be modified and be willing to adjust.

- Not everyone can benefit from a specific morning or daily routine. You must remain aware, think positively, and be prepared to adjust so you can develop the most beneficial practices.

- Don't use this Life Ground Rule to justify a lack of effort or failures.

- Just because no one thing works for everyone, remain self-aware to ensure you don't subconsciously use this as an excuse— "it just doesn't work for me."

- Some things will be more challenging for others to learn, acquire or perform. So put in the work and earn your way. Take what you've learned and adjust it to you. Don't water it down. Modify it to make it better for you.

- The only exceptions are Meditation, Affirmations and Visualization.

- Everyone should and can benefit from some form of Meditation to ease and center the mind.

- Those who say they can't meditate or say that it doesn't work for them, need it the most.

- Everyone should and can benefit from creating their own affirmations and stating them periodically, if not daily.

LIFE GROUND RULES

- Stating affirmations is one of the best ways to self-motivate and inspire. When practiced consistently, affirmations help adjust the subconscious mind.

- Everyone should and can benefit from Visualization. You must see it in your mind first before it becomes a reality. Remember, everything starts with a thought.

- In all things, take ownership and responsibility, and find what works for you. Then, do the work and find your path.

- To accomplish anything worthwhile in life, sacrifice, hard work, discipline, and consistency cannot be avoided. Balanced consistency is key!

To be yourself in a world that is constantly trying to make you something else is the greatest accomplishment.

— **Ralph Waldo Emerson**

LIFE GROUND RULES

Ownership & Action

Excuses are a time thief. Have a goal, accept responsibility, and take action!

— **Steve Maraboli**

As humans, we have gotten soft and weak, especially those of us living in first-world countries. By first-world, I'm referring to economically stable, industrialized countries whose citizens enjoy and expect a high standard of living. In such current environments, things have become easy. For most of us, food, water, clothing, shelter, information, and opportunities are readily available. For some, these things may be harder to obtain but not impossible. As we close out the Information Age and enter the Experience Age, we are no longer in a survival-of-the-fittest world. Most of us no longer worry about having to hunt and gather food or about building a shelter. We no longer struggle to ensure we have enough clothing to protect us from the elements. Instead, we are more concerned with what restaurant delivers food, the brand names we wear, and whether the colors of our clothes match. This shift, where most of us are more concerned with fashion than with our physical survival, has made us comfy. Fast food, technology and social media have made things more problematic. Some have gotten too comfortable. To the point that we lack drive and have become weak in mind and body.

In our current world, most don't have to be strong and smart to survive. If that were the case, many would suffer and perish. Consequently, there is little to no incentive to stay healthy and fit and improve our knowledge base. And with technology, we don't even have to adjust our bad habits to survive and thrive. We can just fake it and put "filters" on everything. Worst yet, social media has made it possible for us to express our opinion and make demands, whatever they may be, without showing face. Because we are weak and sensitive, many choose to hide behind their screens to rant and insult people with impunity. The weak have become bold because they can hide and still reach the masses. So, not only have we become weak, soft, and overly sensitive, but we have also acquired a false sense of bravery and security. This has created a cozy environment where the fainthearted can survive and thrive.

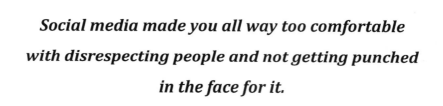

Social media made you all way too comfortable with disrespecting people and not getting punched in the face for it.

— **Mike Tyson**

Although we collectively have gotten soft and comfortable, the fact remains that life is hard and can be complicated. On some occasions, life is not fair and perhaps difficult. Yet, regardless of our dilemmas, it is ultimately up to us to fix them. If you want to overcome any obstacle, regardless of who or what created the problem, the first step towards resolving it is to take ownership. This may sound harsh and unreasonable, but it is the truth. Why? Because either no one cares or no one can truly help you with what's going on inside of you or around you. When many come face-to-face with this realization for the first time, they crumble. So, it is best to accept it now and be mentally prepared for upcoming issues. Understand that besides the superficial, "I hope everything turns out well for you" or "we'll keep you in our thoughts and prayers," most people really don't care or can't help. On rare occasions that your problems cause others to be empathetic, it is usually for a limited amount of time. And although some of the closest people to you may be concerned, few are willing to assist, and fewer are able to provide aid. They may care for you, but they too, are dealing with their individual challenges. For life is hard and stops for no one. Finally, there are those who genuinely love you. They can provide aid, and in most cases, the best they can do is assist and comfort you for some time. But, at some point, you'll have to take ownership and help yourself. Because no one will continue to help someone who is not willing to help themselves. Consequently, at the end of the day, it is up to you to accept responsibility and do the work required to repair or improve things in your life.

Friends, Family & Distractions

There are some, but few, who have friends and family members who can assist during difficulties. If you are one of these, understand that you are fortunate. Never forget to thank them. And always show appreciation to those who support you during dark times. This is a rare advantage. True friends and caring family members should never be taken for granted. Yet don't be offended or take it personally when people close to you are unable to help during tough times. Recognize that everyone is dealing with their own issues and problems. Everyone deals with internal or external demons. That is everyone, no one excluded. And, to avoid dealing with our shortcomings and inner terrors, most of us unconsciously seek distractions. We seek things that make us forget or blind to the difficult truth facing us. We rather think about other things or do anything else but that which must be done. And one of the biggest distractions today is social media.

When trying to complete a task, over half of all adults with smart devices are distracted by social media to some degree or another. And the statistics for teenagers are worst. Additionally, studies have shown that the heavy use of social media fosters low self-esteem and makes some feel insufficient. The tragedy is that most things on social media are not what they appear to be. Therefore, spending too much time on social media wastes time, and one can end up feeling down. For those reasons, don't allow yourself to be misled by people who use filters and alterations to appear like they live perfect lives. Because those who really live a good life don't brag and display it in that manner. Many on social media display great experiences. But they only show you the good times, and obviously, no one lives an extraordinary life all the time. The truth is that life, at times, can be difficult, complicated and unfair for us all. But that part is not displayed and glorified.

In addition to life being unfair and challenging, we must also deal with Human Polarity. Understand that when facing difficult times, if we continue to focus on the problem and the negative, we run the risk of mutating into an antagonistic villain. The villain in us will only make things worse. If we focus too much on the demons we struggle with, we too can become a demon. Due to Human Polarity, without awareness, we can turn a bad situation into a living nightmare. So, we cannot let our problems define who we are. We must not allow difficult times to get the best of us. The best way to do this is to accept the facts and stop making excuses.

Once people stop making excuses, stop blaming others, and take ownership of everything in their lives, they are compelled to take action to solve their problems.

— Jocko Willink

Accept & Take Ownership

We must accept that we have gotten soft and comfortable in a world where life can be unfair and, at times, brutal. We must also acknowledge and understand that no one is coming to help or liberate us. There is no rescue team on the way because certain parts of life's journey must be walked alone. Therefore, there is no use in continuing to complain about our hardships since no one can really help. In fact, if we always expect someone to help, this worsens the situation in the long run. The temporary help we receive becomes an enabler as we become weaker and more dependent. So we are left with no other choice. If we want to change or improve anything in life, we must take ownership of the issues. Once we accept and take ownership of our life, we can then take the initiative and make things happen.

During tough times, making things happen requires courage, not excuses. It demands action, not justifications. This also means that if there is a problem, we can't ignore it because it will get worst. Regardless of what it is, if you see a problem, you own it. You must own your life; the good, the bad, and the ugly, without excuses. You must take personal ownership of yourself and the trajectory of your life. This point can't be repeated enough. Improving and further developing anything in life requires taking ownership.

During the process of taking ownership, one gains knowledge of self. This is the first step— awareness. As we get acquainted with ourselves and our surroundings, we gain knowledge that helps us better understand the obstacles ahead. Once we comprehend who we are, our environment, and the challenges, we can start to seek solutions. We then find and implement solutions without advertising them to the world. We move in silence without publicizing our intentions. We simply become aware, we learn, and we act. It is a simple yet effective formula; gain the knowledge and implement it.

In many cases, knowledge is power. Yet in life, knowledge, in and of itself, is not enough. This is proven by the fact that although we are in the digital age and have access to all the information we will ever need, we continue to struggle with all aspects of life. Moreover, despite having all the information at our fingertips, we still have a hard time applying it. Thus, in life, knowledge is not power. Because unless we act to apply what we know, we remain powerless.

Therefore, knowledge is not power, but rather, the practical application of knowledge is true power. Taking action to apply what we've learned is crucial to get the desired result. Nothing happens without action. Action is king. The ground rule of *Ownership & Action* states that acceptance is necessary and is the first step to changing or improving anything. Once we accept and take ownership, we must follow up with deeds.

We must take action to make things happen. The Law of Attraction, without action, is worthless. Because taking action is the only thing that will initiate change. Consistent action is better because it makes it possible to improve and achieve goals. Taking precise actions consistently is best because it will change your life. This *Ground Rule* applies to everything in life– big or small. It doesn't matter what you know or think. Accepting ownership and taking action is what works.

The Life Ground Rule of *Ownership & Action* is best explained by Jim Rohn, who said, "*If you want to have more, you have to become more. For things to change, you have to change. For things to get better, you have to become better. If you improve, everything will improve for you. If you grow, your money will grow; your relationships, your health, your business, and every external effect will mirror that growth in equal correlation*".

This quote best describes how we must accept and take possession of our situation, understanding that things will only change and improve based on our decisions and actions. This explanation is simple and accurate yet challenging for some to acknowledge. The difficulty lies in the realization that it is up to us, as individuals, to make things happen for ourselves and our environment. We only gain control of our lives when we comprehend that responsibility has no escape and action has no substitute.

Once acknowledged, this philosophy, which places all burdens on our shoulders, is easy to understand. Yet the possibility of failure still makes it difficult to implement. It's an uncomfortable feeling to admit that we are solely responsible for our own success or failure. This mindset eliminates anyone else or anything else to blame. It also removes dozens of so-called legitimate reasons to justify not being able to take action. In addition to that, once we take ownership and begin to act, there is no guarantee that we will prosper or when we will succeed. Remember, life is complicated and unfair, so success is not guaranteed to anyone, but failure is. Therefore, we have no choice but to try. We try until we fail because without failure, there is no growth. We learn from our failures, adjust if we must, and continue trying until we reach our destination.

Action is the foundational key to all success.

Pablo Picasso

Play To Win

I don't want to play; I want to win. But if you give me the rules, I'll take it from there.

— **Veronica Rossi**

I f you were to research and look for this information, you will find it. This is not newly discovered information. But it may take you some time to locate all of it because it is scattered through different sources. Or, simply by remaining aware while living your life and through your personal experiences, you will discover these truths on your own. It may take some time, but you will eventually come to the same understanding. As I previously said, this is nothing new. All I did was gather and place this information in one easy-to-read book. I hope that having this information now will save you time and hard aches. I am convinced that applying this knowledge will enrich some parts of your life.

I have personally found these *Life Ground Rules* to be powerful and extremely useful in many aspects of my life. I am convinced that they can be beneficial to you as well. Yet these *Ground Rules* can only work to the degree that you understand and employ them. These concepts work, but you must fully comprehend them, recognize when to use them and be consistent with how you apply them. In order to fully understand, recognize and be effective with your consistency, you may have to read the book several times. Not hard to do because it's a short read. This was purposely done with that in mind. You can conveniently read, learn and understand. Then you'll be able to use and apply these rules where they best suit you. Once you know and understand the *Life Ground Rules*, go out in the world, and play smarter, not harder. Play to win. For winners understand and apply these four *Life Ground Rules*.

- Human Energy: Energy is everything, and everything is energy. Including in your mind, body and spirit. In your body, as it relates to what is required for systems to function, the brain uses the most energy. This is so because everything starts with a thought. A thought initiates the mind-body energy chain. This "chain" is what moves us from thought to action. So be conscious of your thoughts and be mindful of the words you use. Especially those words that repeat themselves in your thoughts. Energy comes in various forms, hard and soft being two forms. Hard and soft energies help establish balance. These two forms of energy also produce their respective skill sets: hard skills and soft skills. Both skill sets are needed to excel and live a wholesome life. Therefore, it benefits us to learn and use both skill sets. Understand that everything we do requires energy.

  Consequently, we must do all that is possible to generate and expand our mental, physical, and spiritual energy. But then, protect your human energy at all costs. Don't let others steal or misuse your energy.

- Human_Polarity: Good and evil live within everyone. Good and evil live within you as well, so don't be naïve. Without awareness and focus, you too can be compromised. We all have inner demons, find yours and control them. Don't focus on the problems, be optimistic and focus on solutions. Focus on the good and the positive and feed the hero within. Constantly make an effort to love and accept everyone but always protect yourself at all times. Come in peace, but be ready for war.

- Same, Yet Different: We are all the same. As in one human race. We are all equal, so stop hating others. However, we are all independently different, so find your individuality. Be real, be you. Consider this *Ground Rule* in all you do, and take responsibility for your mental, physical, and spiritual health. Don't just freely accept the words or advice of others without considering your individuality.

- Ownership & Action: Life sometimes sucks. It can be challenging and unfair. Additionally, at times it seems like no one cares. So what? You are strong; if not, make yourself strong. Meditate, exercise, and create a Focus Session to make you mentally, physically, and spiritually tough. With strength, you can take ownership of the problems facing you. This strength also allows you to take the actions necessary to change and improve things. Nothing outside of who you are can change you or make your life better. No one and nothing outside of your mind, body, and spirit can make you more intelligent or prosperous. Everything we need and the answers we seek are locked within us. Everything is within you. And the key is accepting ownership of your life and taking the necessary actions to make things happen.

Now that you have the *Ground Rules* for life, in Book 2, we will explore the *Purpose and Meaning of Life*.

The End

It requires wisdom to understand wisdom: the
music is nothing if the audience is deaf.

Walter Lippmann

About the Series

Greatness consists of having a genuine desire and a good purpose, it is not a one time battle, but a lifelong habit.

— Kidadl

In my early 40s, after accomplishing most of my lifelong goals, I went through a challenging period. I began to ask myself, "What now?". It was one of those experiences where you start to second-guess yourself and doubt everything. I questioned the purpose and meaning of life. As I wandered through life, I didn't care as much. I let myself go, mentally and physically. This resulted in the deterioration of my health. After getting tired of feeling sick and empty, I decided to do something about it. I spend the next three years reading, researching and exploring. I applied what I learned and tried different things. I interviewed doctors and conducted experiments on myself. This is when I coined the phrase "optimistic seeker" and tried hard to live through this persona. Because despite failures, I was determined and continued to seek, optimistically. As I learned, one thing led me to another, which expanded my outlook on things. In the end, with the help of many, I found what I was looking for, and my health was restored. I now know that not having Direction and Balance initiated or caused my troubles.

Going through these difficulties humbled me, and I learned a great deal. Besides understanding the importance of Direction and Balance, I became aware that health is not just about being fit. To be completely healthy requires an active and holistic approach. I also discovered that many go through similar experiences. This motivated me to share my experiences and knowledge with others. I realized that other people could benefit from this information if they knew how to apply it. Sharing this information became a desire and then a life purpose. At first, I wasn't sure exactly how I would do it, but I called this purpose, Empowering the Mind, Body, and Spirit (Empowering MBS).

With time, my life purpose became more apparent and specific. It then transformed into a specific goal; *"to serve and empower others by speaking and writing."* I then began to document everything I learned through this experience and in life. Both through my successes and my many failures. This gave birth to what I eventually called The EMBS Systematic Process. By documenting my experiences and the lessons learned, I developed an organized method to identify obstacles that hold us back in life and ways to overcome them. This process became the tool I used to share my philosophy and techniques with the world. By sharing these teachings, I intend to **empower** others and save them unnecessary pain, time and effort. I am not saying that this process will solve all your problems. But I am confident that whoever applies these principles will come closer to the successful, happy and fulfilled life they are searching for and want to establish.

The Process

The EMBS Systematic Process is an all-inclusive, self-improvement and personal-development curriculum. It is like a workout program for your entire life. The process includes a complete, step-by-step, and effective course of action with easy-to-understand concepts, practical techniques and no-nonsense tools and resources. The concepts and techniques are specifically designed to inspire, guide, track and focus on personal growth efforts. These principles, when applied, help individuals reach their full potential.

The EMBS Systematic Process takes big, "in the clouds" thoughts and ideas and transforms them into techniques that can be practically applied in your daily life. These are not just loose theories and ideas. These are things that you can actually do and implement into your life to improve and become better. But you must be willing to learn, apply and be consistent.

Like Many of You

Like many of you, I read books and listened to great motivational speakers who inspired me. Yet once I was inspired, I was always left guessing... OK, what now? What do I do next? How do I start, and how do I apply this inspiration to my life? The EMBS Systematic Process answers those questions. It moves you from inspiration to knowledge and from knowledge to practical application. I learned the hard way that knowledge, in and of itself, is not power. But rather, the practical application of knowledge is true power. The EMBS Systematic Process provides practical knowledge and shows you how YOU can *empower* yourself to reach your personal greatness. This is not a gimmick. Remember that old-fashioned hard work and commitment produce great things, and great things take time. The EMBS Systematic Process works, but it requires time and effort.

KEYS TO GREATNESS

To present what I learned to the world, I wrote my first book, *The Optimistic Seekers' Keys to Greatness: A Guide to Establishing a Successful, Happy, and Fulfilled Life.* In my first attempt as an author, I tried to cover my entire philosophy and everything I learned in a single book. As you can imagine, it was a relatively large book. This did not appeal to the masses, especially in an age where most have developed a shorter attention span. So, I updated and "remixed" what I wrote and divided it into smaller, digestible chunks. As a result, I create a book series consisting of well-organized mini books, The KEYS TO GREATNESS book series.

Greatness is not a destination; it is a continuous journey that never ends.

— **Brad Lomenick**

This book series approach allows readers to learn and apply a set of techniques at a time without feeling overwhelmed with the entire curriculum. I also created a Course for each book in the series. The Courses provide more in-depth information with visuals and audio.

A joint book-and-course system provides all individuals an opportunity to acquire and be reminded of this knowledge, regardless of their preferred learning method. This combined approach offers practical life lessons that are applicable to the real world. The series was created for those who want more out of life and are willing to learn along their journey and for Optimistic Seekers.

Optimistic Seeker

An Optimistic Seeker is a dynamic and ambitious person who takes ownership and responsibility for their life. Optimistic Seekers are willing to get out of their comfort zone and are ready to try new things. They are eager to take new approaches so they can change or improve their current conditions.

Optimistic Seekers understand that life is complicated and can be difficult. They also recognize that during some difficulties, we fail. Yet, despite failures, Optimistic Seekers do not quit. Instead, they learn from their failures. In doing so, they become self-aware and develop a strong, positive mindset. And when faced with future difficulties, Optimistic Seekers take a warrior-monk approach to withstand defeats, overcome obstacles, and achieve goals.

Optimistic Seekers desire more out of life, and they want to enrich their experiences. But more importantly, they are willing to put in the consistent hard work required to reach their goals. By being consistent, Optimistic Seekers develop new habits and diligently become self-empowered as they continue to learn, grow and enjoy their life journey.

Optimism is essential to achievement and it is also the foundation of courage and true progress.

— **Nicholas M. Butler**

About the Author

Accept, forgive, let go, and surrender. Be honest and be patient. Establish Direction and maintain Balance. Love everyone and everything. Come in peace but be ready for war. Do not judge, gossip, get angry or frustrated. Instead, be good, be kind, and be happy. Speak less, listen more, and love deeply. Above all else, Focus and move forward.

— Joel Rodriguez, *The Optimistic Seeker*

Joel Rodriguez was born and raised in The South Bronx, New York, during the 1980s heroin and crack cocaine epidemic. By age sixteen, he was a high school dropout and labeled an underprivileged, troubled, and at-risk youth. Defying the odds, Joel rose out of poverty, became a U.S. Marine, and established a career in federal law enforcement. Joel Rodriguez held several positions as a law enforcement professional. He has traveled extensively throughout the United States and abroad and is an avid reader of self-improvement and personal development books.

Despite his accomplishments, Joel has also faced personal challenges and life difficulties. Yet through perseverance, research, exploring, and conducting experiments on himself, Joel overcame several devastating life obstacles. Then, by applying what he learned, he drastically improved and revolutionized his life. During this process, Joel developed a new way of thinking and life philosophy. Wanting to share this mindset and philosophy with the world, he became a speaker and an author and established Empowering Mind, Body & Spirit (Empowering MBS).

Empowering MBS is a self-improvement and personal development lifestyle company that uses an action-based and holistic approach to restore and transform lives. Empowering MBS offers practical training and tools to *empower* individuals who want more out of life and are willing to do the work. As an author, Joel Rodriguez's KEYS TO GREATNESS book series and Courses are formatted to inspire, guide, track and focus on self-improvement efforts and personal development goals. Each book and Course provide easy-to-understand concepts and practical techniques. Joel Rodriguez is not a "guru." Instead, he is a resilient man with a wide range of experiences, some successes and many, many failures. The failures and difficulties that he endured resulted in hard lessons learned. These tough lessons forced him to change and adapt to a new way of thinking. He now shares these practical life lessons with the world. Joel's goal is to serve and empower others by speaking and writing. Empowering MBS is the vehicle he uses to achieve this goal. Utilizing Empowering MBS as a platform, combined with his experiences and people skills, Joel Rodriguez, The Optimistic Seeker, connects with individuals and small audiences seeking to improve their lives and reach their full potential.

Empowering MBS is a self-improvement and personal development lifestyle company that uses an action-based and holistic; mind, body, and spirit approach.

— **Joel Rodriguez,** *The Optimistic Seeker*

GUIDING SUCCESS -
ESTABLISHING GREATNESS

As long as we live, our journey continues. There are always things to learn, experiences to try, places to visit, people to meet and new goals to pursue. If you are not taking this approach in life, you are not living.

— Joel Rodriguez, *The Optimistic Seeker*

Even if we remain flexible, we need ground rules.

— **Horst Seehofer**

KEYS TO GREATNESS
by Joel Rodriguez

"Please leave a kind review and share this information with others. Together, we can empower more individuals looking to self-improve and develop. Like, share and follow me on social media. For information, visit EmpoweringMBS. com. Thank you."

LIFE GROUND RULES

Made in the USA
Middletown, DE
29 October 2022

13742594R00049